MATTEO PERICOLI

LONDON for CHILDREN

NORTH BANK

MACMILLAN CHILDREN'S BOOKS

FOREWORD by MATTEO PERICOLI

Cities are big! Look at London, isn't it big?

I like cities and I like to draw. So when I saw London I wanted to draw it — and that's exactly what I did. But drawing a city isn't easy because it's hard to know where to start or where to end and there are so many decisions to make. So I came up with a plan to walk along the banks of the Thames and, from each side, take photos of the other side. I decided that whatever I saw of the city from the river, that's what I would draw. No choosing, just everything. And in drawing it all I knew I could also tell a story.

London is so big and so beautiful that the idea of capturing the north and south banks was very exciting to me, and the drawings I made are inside this book. But they are not alone because the Thames has its very own story to tell. Do you know how many things in British history have happened on or near this river? How much history and information it holds? Well, more than can ever possibly fit inside this book! But thanks to the help of the wonderful people at Macmillan, on every page there is something exciting and interesting to read so that you too can discover some of London's story — and find out more about the *everything* I drew.

You will encounter lots of fun things: plagues, pirates and princes in towers, brilliant buildings, beautiful pageants and big explosions. There is so much here to discover and I hope you will see one thing right away: That drawing *everything* may be more tiring than just drawing *something*, but it is so much more fun!

Matteo

MY ORIGINAL DRAWINGS MEASURE 12 METRES LONG EACH - SO LONG THAT THEY COULDNT EVEN FIT IN THIS BOOK.

TO CREATE THEM I WALKED ALMOST 40 MILES! FROM HAMMERSMITH BRIDGE ALL THE WAY TO THE O2 IN GREENWICH. AND I DID THIS ON BOTH SIDES OF THE THAMES.

IT TOOK ME 2 WEEKS AND I WALKED SO FAR MY SHOES CRACKED AND BROKE.

I TOOK MORE THAN 6,000 PICTURES OF THE THAMES. IMAGINE: IF YOU WERE TO TAKE ONE PHOTO AN HOUR, YOU WOULD BE PHOTOGRAPHING FOR 250 DAYS! OR IMAGINE THIS: IF YOU WERE TO TAKE ONE PHOTOGRAPH A DAY IT WOULD TAKE YOU 16 & A HALF YEARS TO TAKE MORE THAN 6,000 PICTURES.

I DREW 3,262 WAVES, 1,343 BUILDINGS, 27,180 WINDOWS, 41 BRIDGES AND 58 CRANES. I KNOW THIS BECAUSE I WAS CRAZY ENOUGH TO COUNT THEM ALL.

The complete NORTH BANK

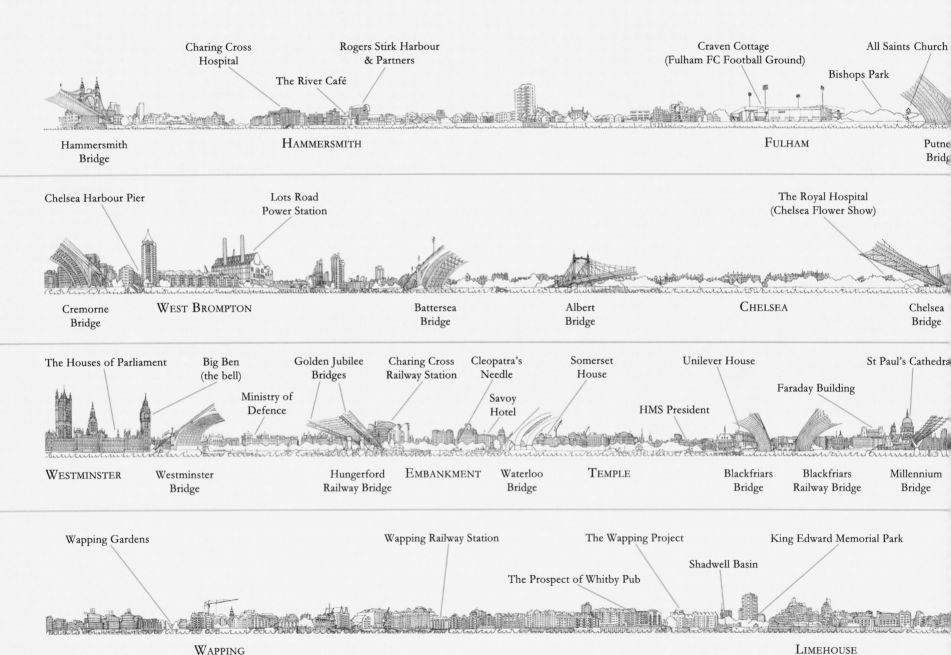

Charing Cross
Hospital

Rogers Stirk Harbour
& Partners

The River Café

Craven Cottage
(Fulham FC Football Ground)

All Saints Church

Bishops Park

Hammersmith
Bridge

HAMMERSMITH

FULHAM

Putney
Bridge

Chelsea Harbour Pier

Lots Road
Power Station

The Royal Hospital
(Chelsea Flower Show)

Cremorne
Bridge

WEST BROMPTON

Battersea
Bridge

Albert
Bridge

CHELSEA

Chelsea
Bridge

The Houses of Parliament

Big Ben
(the bell)

Golden Jubilee
Bridges

Charing Cross
Railway Station

Cleopatra's
Needle

Somerset
House

Unilever House

St Paul's Cathedral

Ministry of
Defence

Savoy
Hotel

Faraday Building

HMS President

WESTMINSTER

Westminster
Bridge

Hungerford
Railway Bridge

EMBANKMENT

Waterloo
Bridge

TEMPLE

Blackfriars
Bridge

Blackfriars
Railway Bridge

Millennium
Bridge

Wapping Gardens

Wapping Railway Station

The Wapping Project

King Edward Memorial Park

The Prospect of Whitby Pub

Shadwell Basin

WAPPING

LIMEHOUSE

MATTEO'S ENTIRE ORIGINAL DRAWING LOOKS LIKE THIS:

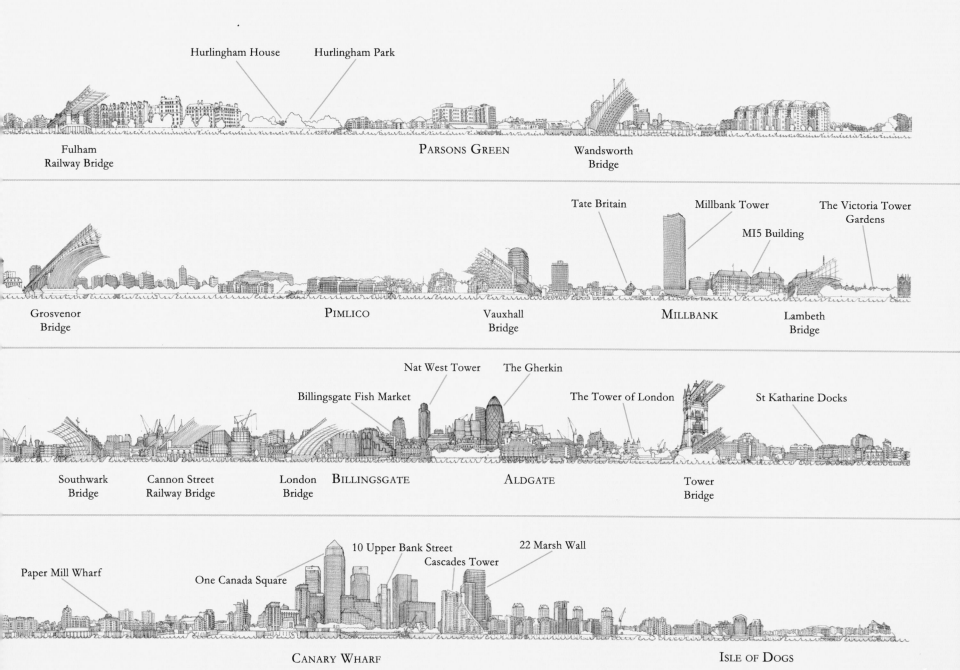

Hurlingham House

Hurlingham Park

Fulham
Railway Bridge

PARSONS GREEN

Wandsworth
Bridge

Tate Britain

Millbank Tower

MI5 Building

The Victoria Tower
Gardens

Grosvenor
Bridge

PIMLICO

Vauxhall
Bridge

MILLBANK

Lambeth
Bridge

Nat West Tower

The Gherkin

Billingsgate Fish Market

The Tower of London

St Katharine Docks

Southwark
Bridge

Cannon Street
Railway Bridge

London
Bridge

BILLINGSGATE

ALDGATE

Tower
Bridge

10 Upper Bank Street

22 Marsh Wall

Cascades Tower

Paper Mill Wharf

One Canada Square

CANARY WHARF

ISLE OF DOGS

We begin our journey along the NORTH BANK here in Pimlico...

At very low tide you can see two wooden posts in the water just across this bridge. They date from before 55 BC and may belong to the earliest known bridge-like structure in London, which led out to an island in the river and was possibly used for burying the dead!

DID YOU KNOW?

If you dig 16 feet below London you'll find an inch-deep layer of black ash. This is the mark left by Queen Boudica, who burnt the city to the ground in a revenge attack on the Romans in 61 AD.

VAUXHALL BRIDGE

In 2006 a baby bottlenose whale swam all the way up the Thames, arriving very near here. It was far from its home in the waters off the north coast of Scotland and sadly it didn't survive the journey back.

Tate Britain

During World War Two the paintings were removed from the Tate Gallery to keep them safe from the bombs. That is, all except one by Sir Stanley Spencer, which was too big to move. So instead they built a brick wall in front of it!

During the war many of the paintings were also stored in nearby Underground stations and disused tunnels.

One of the things London is most famous for is the 'London Underground' – a network of railway tunnels connecting 270 stations and including 402 km of track. It opened in 1863 and was the first of its kind in the world; today the only larger one is in Shanghai, China.

THE GUNPOWDER PLOT

In 1605 a group of Catholics planned to blow up the House of Lords during its state opening, to kill the Protestant King James I and most of the country's most important men. The plot failed because an anonymous warning was sent to one of the Lords, who showed it to the King. The House of Lords was searched and Guy Fawkes was discovered in a cellar with matches and thirty-six barrels of gunpowder!

THE GREAT STINK

In the hot summer of 1858 the smell of the sewage that flowed into the Thames was so unbearable that Parliament draped huge curtains, soaked in bleach, over the roofs to cloak the smell and get rid of the germs. The sewage in the Thames had been getting worse and allowing disease to spread. But it was only the disgusting smell of the Great Stink that forced them into action, and plans for the finest sewer system in the world were put in place.

Lambeth Bridge

Guy Fawkes tried to hide his identity by insisting his name was John Johnson. Shame he couldn't think of a better name – his plan was uncovered and he was tortured in the Tower and then executed.

THE
HOUSES
— OF —
PARLIAMENT

These were
burned down
in 1834, when
someone left
a fire burning
in the cellar
all night and
it spread to
the rest of the
building.

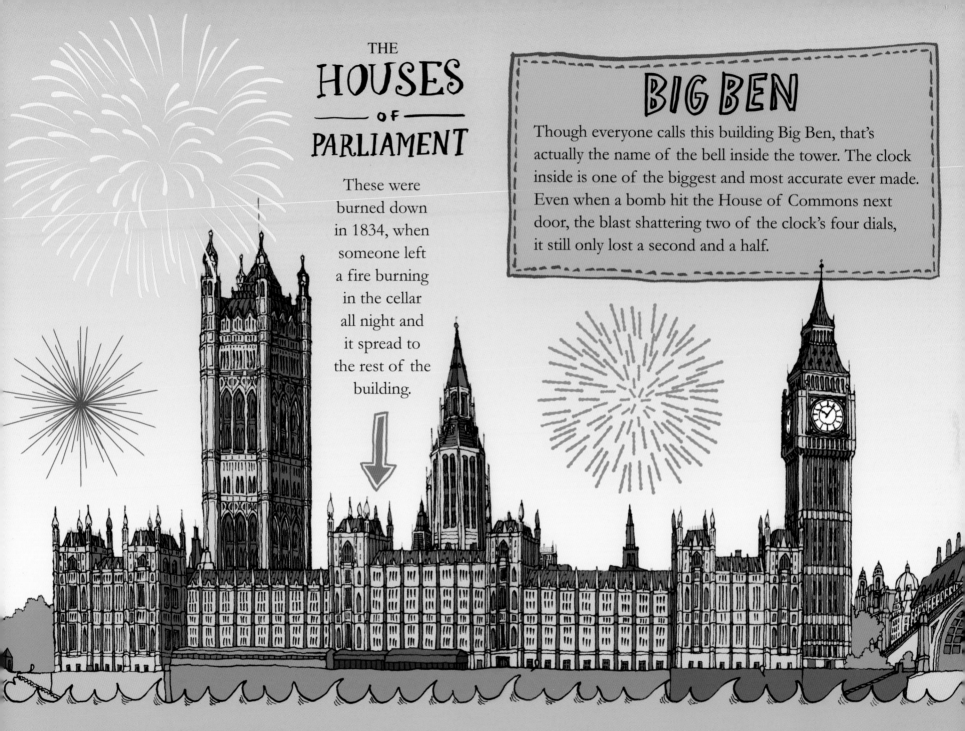

BIG BEN

Though everyone calls this building Big Ben, that's
actually the name of the bell inside the tower. The clock
inside is one of the biggest and most accurate ever made.
Even when a bomb hit the House of Commons next
door, the blast shattering two of the clock's four dials,
it still only lost a second and a half.

FLOOD
Before the embankments were built the Thames used to flood regularly. One of the worst floods was in 1816
when it was said that men rowed through the great hall of Westminster, and that when the waters subsided the
floor was covered with dead fish!

WESTMINSTER BRIDGE

This bridge is painted green to match the colour of the chairs inside the House of Commons.

BEER EXPLOSION

In 1814 a huge vat of beer exploded in a brewery off the Tottenham Court Road. It blew up the vat next to it, and that one blew up another. In all nearly 1.5 million litres of beer spilled out into the street! But it wasn't a treat for the locals as many people nearby lived in cellar rooms, which flooded, and eight people drowned in beer!

Taxi!

In order to drive one of London's famous black cabs, drivers have to take a gruelling test called The Knowledge, where they memorise all the important routes through the city so they never have to stop and look at a map!

SMALL BEER anyone?

From the Middle Ages until the 19th century it was much safer to drink beer than water, because the water in beer had been boiled during the brewing process, killing dangerous bacteria.

Even children drank beer, often for breakfast! This drink was known as 'small beer' because it contained very little alcohol.

HUNGERFORD Bridge

CLEOPATRA'S
NEEDLE

This was given to the British in 1819, but was so impossible to move that it was thought to be a joke gift! It remained in Egypt for more than sixty years. Eventually a metal pontoon was built for it, but a storm struck during the voyage and it was believed to have sunk. However, Spanish fishermen rescued it and four days later it arrived in London. This sculpture didn't actually belong to Cleopatra (who died in 30 BC), but to the earlier Egyptian ruler Tuthmosis III. It was already a thousand years old when Cleopatra was alive!

There is a time capsule buried beneath it, containing objects from 1878, including children's toys, daily newspapers, a set of coins, a map of London and twelve photographs showing the best-looking English women of the day. (Queen Victoria's photo was apparently hastily added before it was buried.)

WATERLOO BRIDGE

SOMERSET HOUSE

Built in 1547-51 as a renaissance palace, this building has been home to a royal family, the Royal Academy, the Royal Society and the Royal Navy, to name but a few! It's now home the Courtauld Institute and Gallery and in winter you can ice skate here.

There are also dancing fountains!

a TALL story

There's a famous tale that the inventor and first wearer of the top hat was John Hetherington, who wore it along the Strand (which runs behind the buildings below) one day in 1797 and caused such a stir that several women fainted! The story goes that he was arrested and charged with starting a riot and fined £500. (But sadly, it's not true.)

HMS PRESIDENT Built as a convoy protection ship for use in World War One.

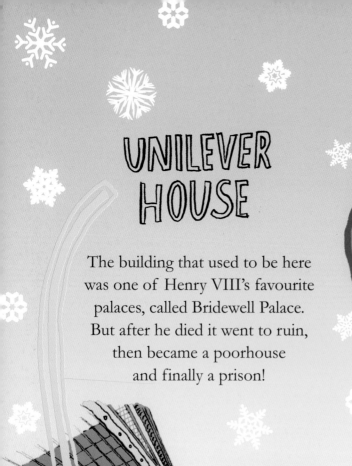

UNILEVER HOUSE

The building that used to be here was one of Henry VIII's favourite palaces, called Bridewell Palace. But after he died it went to ruin, then became a poorhouse and finally a prison!

FREEZE

Between about 1550 and 1850, Britain experienced a 'Little Ice Age' when temperatures were often so cold that the Thames would freeze over. In the 1660s 'frost fairs' were held on the frozen river, complete with tents, stalls, merry-go-rounds, football matches and even ice bowling.

Henry VIII is also said to have travelled on the river by sleigh from Westminster to Greenwich during a big freeze.

BLACKFRIARS BRIDGE

BLACKFRIARS RAILWAY BRIDGE

In 1814 an elephant was led across the frozen Thames here by Blackfriars bridge, to prove to people it was safe to cross by foot.

St Paul's

There has been a cathedral on this site since the 7th century – more than 1,400 years. The cathedral we see today was designed by Sir Christopher Wren after the old one burned down in the Great Fire of London in 1666 (more about the fire on the next page!).

Amazingly the building that stood here before was even bigger (see outline), even though it was built in the 12th century.

ONE DOME or THREE

When you stand inside St Paul's and look up you see the first domed roof, but there are actually two more above this one. The interior roof is lower, to look more appropriate from the inside, but more domes were added to make St Paul's taller, and a more impressive sight on the London skyline.

Millennium Bridge

Prince Charles and Lady Diana were married in St Paul's.

The GREAT FIRE OF LONDON

The Great Fire of 1666 started in a bakery on Pudding Lane. Four days later almost all of the city of London had been destroyed. The city's population was 80,000 and more than 70,000 people lost their homes. The whole experience was written down by the greatest diarist of his day, Samuel Pepys (pronounced 'peeps'), who also described how he dug a hole in his back garden to hide his gold, his wine, and his expensive Parmesan cheese.

DID YOU KNOW?

Sir Christopher Wren was given the task of helping to rebuild the city. St Paul's Cathedral is his greatest achievement, but he was also in charge of building fifty churches to replace those that had burnt down. After the fire, buildings were built out of brick and stone rather than flamable wood.

A few days after the fire was extinguished, Pepys was walking along a burnt-out street when he saw a cat being pulled out of the burning rubble of a destroyed house. All its fur was singed off, but it was still alive!

SOUTHWARK BRIDGE

LONDON ORIGINATED HERE!

The Romans settled here in the 1st century AD and named the place 'Londinium'.

London Bridge

There has been a bridge here since the Romans arrived, making it possibly the oldest bridge in the world.

No wonder 'London Bridge is falling down' became a popular rhyme – the bridge has burned down or been destroyed many times: in 1014, 1091 and 1136, when it was just made of wood. It was rebuilt in stone in 1176. But the fires didn't stop there. The only reason the bridge survived the Great Fire of 1666 was because half of it had already burned away in 1633!

Cannon Street Railway Bridge

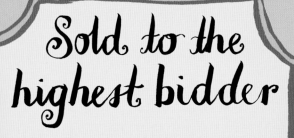

Sold to the highest bidder

In 1967 London Bridge was sold to a businessman in Arizona. It was taken down brick by brick, shipped over to America and rebuilt in a place called Lake Havasu City, where it's now a tourist attraction.

A MASSIVE BOMB

For a long time the tallest building in the UK (until the big tower in Canary Wharf was built in 1990), the NatWest Tower was the target of a huge IRA bomb in 1993. The tower was so badly damaged that the owners wanted to knock it down, but it was so big that it couldn't be pulled down safely. They had to repair it very slowly, very carefully and very expensively – it cost of more than £1 billion.

 Billingsgate Fish Market stood here until 1982. The market was famous for three things: fish (obviously), the distinctive leather hats worn by the fishmongers, and their bad language . . .

THE GHERKIN

Aside from looking like a funny vegetable,
the Gherkin is an amazingly modern and
environmentally friendly design: the way air travels
round the building means it keeps itself warm in
winter and cools itself in summer, and uses half
the energy of other buildings its size.

THE TOWER OF LONDON

Built in the 1070s, the Tower of London has been a castle, a palace and a prison. For centuries it was home to the kings and queens of England. Two of the most tragic residents were the boy princes Edward V and Richard, Duke of York. They were imprisoned by their uncle, who declared himself King Richard III. The boys went missing and are thought to have been murdered and buried on the grounds – the skeletons of two boys were found in 1675, buried under a staircase.

STOP, THIEF!

In 1671 an Irish desperado called Captain Blood stole the crown jewels. Blood was captured but refused to speak to anyone except King Charles II, who was so impressed by Blood's boldness that he released him and gave him lands and an allowance of £500 a year!

Ravens of the Tower

It is said that if the famous ravens ever left the Tower, it would fall and Britain with it. (In fact the birds' wings are clipped very carefully so they can't fly away.)

From the 13th century there was an animal menagerie at the Tower with lions, leopards, an elephant and even a polar bear, which was a gift from the King of Norway. With a chain around its neck, the polar bear was allowed to catch fish for itself from the Thames.

At night Tower Bridge works on the same system as a pedestrian crossing: red light for stop, green light for go. When there was a fog (which used to be very often in London), bells would be used to let ships know whether it was safe to pass through or not.

St Katharine Dock

In 1825-28, when the city was building these docks, 10,000 people were evicted from their homes, with no compensation!

THE LONDON DOCKS

The docks were often named after the things that were delivered there, or where the ships had travelled from. There were docks called Greenland, Russia, Norway or Canada Dock, and the buildings in them were named after cinnamon, cardamom, coriander, ginger, tamarind, vanilla, sesame, caraway and cumin. So much food arrived in London this way that the docks were often referred to as 'London's larder'.

By 1880 London was the busiest port in the world, with more docks being built all the time. There were so many ships waiting to unload their cargo that the river was often jammed with boats queuing to dock, which lasted for days and days!

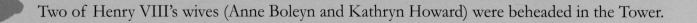

Two of Henry VIII's wives (Anne Boleyn and Kathryn Howard) were beheaded in the Tower.

HANGED, DRAWN and QUARTERED

Being hanged, drawn and quartered is one of the worst punishments in history and it was meted out to Guy Fawkes and his conspirators in the Gunpowder Plot. It was the punishment for committing treason (being disloyal to the ruler or government), but it was only used on men – women were burned at the stake.

First the condemned man was tied to a wooden hurdle and dragged to the place of execution, then hanged until he was nearly dead. He was then taken down, drawn, or disembowelled, (his guts cut open and pulled out) while still alive, and then chopped into pieces (quartered). The pieces were often displayed in a public place.

Guy Fawkes managed to jump from the scaffold, breaking his neck and cheating the executioner. But his body was still drawn and quartered and his body parts put on public display.

DID YOU KNOW?

The day after Buckingham Palace was bombed in World War Two, the Queen Mother came here to meet real victims of bombing. "I'm glad we have been bombed," she said. "Now I can look the East End in the face."

WAPPING GARDENS

Back in the 17th century when this was still countryside, Charles I hunted a stag all the way from North London and killed it near here.

Wapping

This area was originally a Saxon settlement and was all marshland until it was drained in the 16th century. It then became a rich meadow before being developed into the London Docks.

DID YOU KNOW?

There are more languages spoken in London than in any other city in the world.

There are 300 of them

THE THAMES TUNNEL

This is the site of the first tunnel to be built under a river anywhere in the world. It is often attributed to Isambard Kingdom Brunel but it was actually built by his father, Mark Brunel. Isambard, who went on to become one of the most famous engineers of all time, worked on the project as assistant engineer and was very nearly drowned by the tunnel collapsing.

The tunnel took nearly twenty years to build and flooded many times, killing lots of people who worked on it. It was finally completed in 1843 and is still used as a railway tunnel today.

You can visit the Brunel Museum, which is just across the water in Rotherhithe.

Have you seen swans on the Thames? Swans were first introduced to Britain in the 12th century by Richard the Lionheart, who brought them from Cyprus.

DID YOU KNOW?

The Thames Tunnel was once a popular tourist attraction with gift shops, live organ music, fortune tellers and dancing monkeys!

It was a masterpiece of engineering, but financially a failure as it was so expensive to build.

APPLES & PEARS

Cockney rhyming slang was invented in the 1840s by the street sellers of London, so they could talk among themselves without customers (or the police) knowing what they were talking about. You can have a go, it's easy – you just need to make up a phrase that rhymes with the word you're trying to disguise:

APPLES AND PEARS = STAIRS
DOG AND BONE = PHONE
BUTCHER'S HOOK = LOOK
TIT for TAT = HAT
AUTUMN LEAF = THIEF
JIM JAR = CAR
DAISY ROOTS = BOOTS
BO-PEEP = SHEEP

"We're now heading into dangerous waters, read on if you dare...

THE PROSPECT OF WHITBY

Along this stretch of river is a pub that was once known as 'The Devil's Tavern' as it was popular with river thieves and smugglers. The pub still has a set of gallows that hang over the water.

JACK the RIPPER

The first serial killer ever recorded, and one of the most bloodcurdling, Jack the Ripper killed six young women in the East End and had the whole city gripped by fear during 1888. Then the murders suddenly stopped – and he was never caught. Some people think he went mad and was imprisoned, or killed himself, perhaps by throwing himself into the Thames.

KING EDWARD MEMORIAL PARK

This was once a busy 19th century fish market.

DID YOU KNOW?

The 18th century explorer, navigator and pioneer Captain James Cook once lived here.

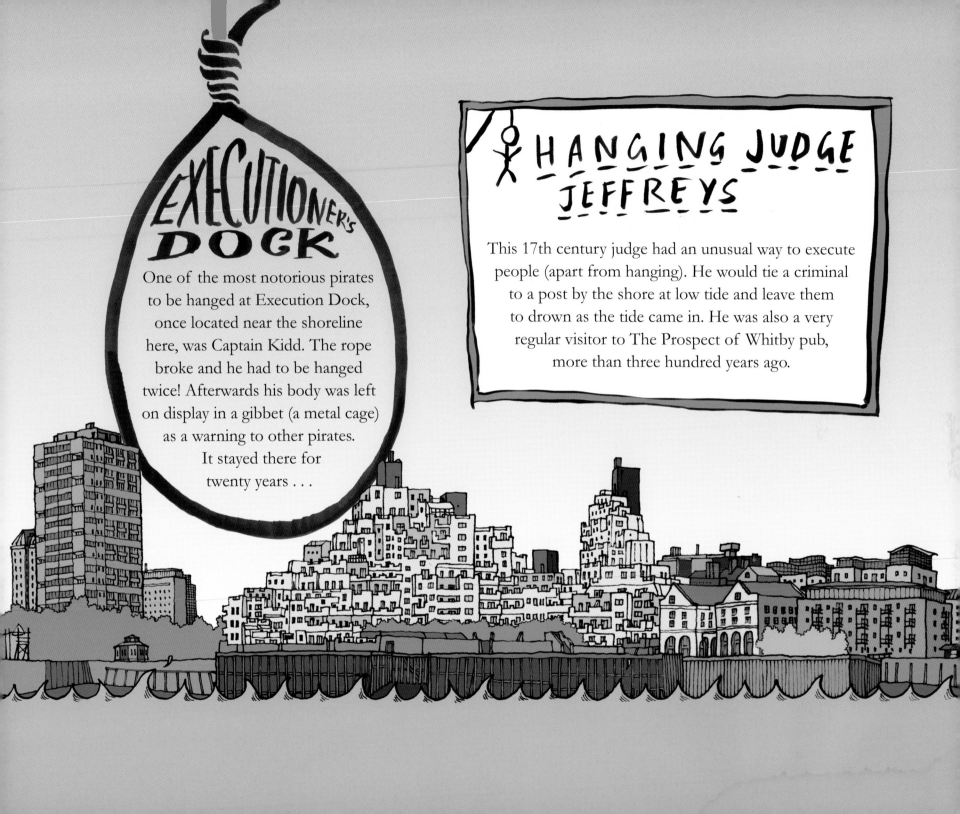

EXECUTIONER's DOCK

One of the most notorious pirates to be hanged at Execution Dock, once located near the shoreline here, was Captain Kidd. The rope broke and he had to be hanged twice! Afterwards his body was left on display in a gibbet (a metal cage) as a warning to other pirates. It stayed there for twenty years . . .

HANGING JUDGE JEFFREYS

This 17th century judge had an unusual way to execute people (apart from hanging). He would tie a criminal to a post by the shore at low tide and leave them to drown as the tide came in. He was also a very regular visitor to The Prospect of Whitby pub, more than three hundred years ago.

River Traffic

The Thames has been a busy working river since Roman times but became even busier during the Industrial Revolution, with the introduction of the Steamboat. The 19th century saw large wooden barges, steamships and paddle steamers mixing with much smaller boats carrying people across the river. These smaller boats were rowed by the Thames watermen.

DID YOU KNOW?

In the 16th century apprentice watermen trained with a master for seven years. They ferried ordinary citizens or rowed private barges for the gentry and nobility, using their expert knowledge of tides and water currents to travel at great speeds. Watermen's stairs can still be seen along the length of the river.

London has more visitors from overseas than any other city – more than 30 million a year!

PAPERMILL WHARF

Hundreds of local women used to sort through waste paper here.

SPRINGHEEL JACK

Long before Jack the Ripper, London was terrorised by Springheel Jack, a mythical half-man, half-monkey who could leap from ground to roof and down again with ease. Many bloodthirsty attacks were blamed on him, although no proof of his existence was ever found.

What a rubbish job!

DID YOU KNOW?

There has been a dock here since Tudor times.

THE ICE AGE

Viewed from above, the Thames begins to curve here and this winding shape was created a long time ago – at the end of the last ice age. The ice caps stretched all the way from the North Pole to just north of here! The river's curved shape was created by meltwaters running off glaciers.

DID YOU KNOW?

Along with New York, London is the world's financial centre.

DID YOU KNOW?

Richard III was the first English monarch to travel to his coronation by water, along the Thames.

London is the 2012 Olympic Games host – the first city to host the games three times (the previous occasions were in 1908 and 1948).

First published 2012 by Macmillan Children's Books
a division of Macmillan Publishers Limited
20 New Wharf Road, London N1 9RR
Basingstoke and Oxford
Associated companies throughout the world
www.panmacmillan.com

Text by Emily Ford and Bruno Vincent
Design by Sharon King Chai

ISBN: 978-1-447-21313-0

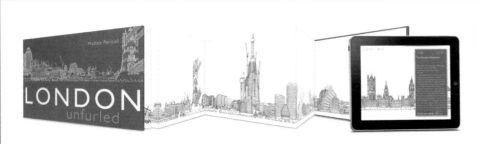